TWO LITTLE MONKEYS JUMPING ON THE BED,
ONE FELL OFF AND BUMPED HIS HEAD.
MOMMY CALLED THE DOCTOR
AND THE DOCTOR SAID,
"NO MORE MONKEYS JUMPING ON THE BED!"

MARY HAD A PRETTY BIRD,
FEATHERS BRIGHT AND YELLOW,
SLENDER LEGS, UPON MY WORD,
HE WAS A PRETTY FELLOW.

ROW, ROW, ROW YOUR BOAT,
GENTLY DOWN THE STREAM.
MERRILY, MERRILY,
MERRILY, MERRILY,
LIFE IS BUT A DREAM.

ONE FOR ME AND ONE FOR YOU,
IF THERE'S ONE LEFT OVER
THEN WHAT'LL WE DO?
TAKE UP A KNIFE AND CUT IT IN TWO
SO THERE'S ONE FOR ME AND ONE FOR YOU.

NIDDLEDY, NODDLEDY, TO AND FRO,
TIRED AND SLEEPY, TO BED WE GO.
JUMP INTO BED, TURN OUT THE LIGHT,
HEAD ON THE PILLOW,
SHUT YOUR EYES TIGHT.

Toddler Time

◆ A Book to Share with Your Toddler ◆

Laurie Krasny Brown

Pictures by Marc Brown

JOY STREET BOOKS

Little, Brown and Company
Boston   Toronto   London

To Eliza, For Your Continuing Inspiration

Special thanks for their generous advice to

Patricia Abelson, parent
Dr. Larry Cohan, parent, pediatrician, and teacher of pediatrics
Tina Craig, nanny and nursery-school teaching assistant
Dr. Ellen Winner, parent and associate professor of
developmental psychology

◆ ◆ ◆

First Edition

Library of Congress Cataloging-in-Publication Data
Brown, Laurene Krasny.
Toddler time: a book to share with your toddler / Laurie Krasny
Brown; pictures by Marc Brown. — 1st ed.
p.   cm.
ISBN 0-316-11263-1
1. Toddlers.   2. Child rearing.   I. Brown, Marc Tolon.
II. Title.
HQ774.5.B76   1990
649'.122 — dc20   90-32342
CIP

Joy Street Books are published by
Little, Brown and Company (Inc.)

10 9 8 7 6 5 4 3 2 1

RAI

Published simultaneously in Canada
by Little, Brown & Company (Canada) Limited

Printed in the United States of America

Between ages one and three, a child takes many dramatic leaps forward in development: he gets up on his own two feet; learns to speak (and say "No!"); begins to pretend; demands to dress himself, feed himself, be the boss (or maybe the baby again); pushes you away, yet loves you more than ever. What do you do? You need more energy, more-watchful eyes, new strategies for recruiting cooperation. It is one of the most challenging times for a parent — and a time when you can profoundly affect your child's emerging sense of self. This is such a special time, and it goes by so quickly. It's Toddler Time!

Laurie Krasny Brown

Contents

Wake-up Time

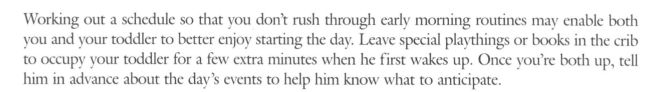

Working out a schedule so that you don't rush through early morning routines may enable both you and your toddler to better enjoy starting the day. Leave special playthings or books in the crib to occupy your toddler for a few extra minutes when he first wakes up. Once you're both up, tell him in advance about the day's events to help him know what to anticipate.

HINTS ◆ Getting up just a bit earlier can make all the difference!

◆ Parents who take their toddler to day care can prepare a lunch box the night before.

4

Dressing

DOODLE, DOODLE, DOO,
THE PRINCESS LOST HER SHOE:
HER HIGHNESS HOPPED;
THE FIDDLER STOPPED,
NOT KNOWING WHAT TO DO.

Toddlers often want to dress themselves before they have the necessary skills. They will struggle through their tears, but you can offer help diplomatically; a toddler may accept help more readily from a stuffed animal willing to start a zipper than from you! By taking the time to acknowledge each tiny accomplishment, you help your toddler to feel proud and independent.

Dressing gives you the perfect chance to identify colors and patterns with your toddler, to talk about weather, to count objects — or simply to admire your child.

HINTS ◆ Provide clothes that are easy to put on and take off; elastic waistbands, big snaps, and Velcro help.

◆ Let your child make some clothes choices.
◆ Humor can turn a dressing task into a silly game.

Meals and Snacks

Try to relax at mealtime. Food preferences change often at this age; a food rejected one day may be accepted a few days later. Keep offering a variety of foods from each of the four basic food groups. Serve small portions; toddlers have small appetites. By discouraging constant snacking, you may help increase a toddler's interest in meals. Instead of making a fuss over food spilled or not eaten, praise your child when he does eat well. Set a good example by your own food choices; foods you enjoy will seem more appealing to your toddler. Remember to bring your sense of humor to the table.

HOT BOILED BEANS
    AND VERY GOOD BUTTER,
LADIES AND GENTLEMEN,
    COME TO SUPPER!

Now is a good time to begin teaching simple manners; encourage your toddler to say "please" and "thank you." Decide what rules about eating are essential — no feet on the table, no talking while you chew, or whatever — and let other things go.

HINTS   Present food in different ways; try arranging a plate of fruit snacks into a face, for example.

◇ Talk about Peter Rabbit and other story characters who like nutritious food such as vegetables.

◇ Let your child make choices, such as between two kinds of juice.

Remember: "Please don't cut it." Okay, I won't.

No cut it!

Here's your porridge, just like Goldilocks!

Mommy, tell me that story.

Tell me, tell me, tell me, please. Shall we count these tasty peas?

Okay, Grammy!

Would you like a star sandwich or a moonwich?

Star!

Can you make a dinosaur sandwich, Dad?

Helping Out

Doing laundry and raking leaves may not excite you, but to your toddler such jobs can be great fun. You may not receive much actual assistance, but a toddler's attempts to help out build his self-esteem. Having pleased you, a toddler feels responsible and more grown up. He practices following simple directions — stir the batter, wipe the table — and improves his manual skills in the process. Forcing cooperation will turn fun into tedium, so don't insist. If you approach chores with a positive attitude, your toddler will too. For now, enjoy your child's willingness to do something for you, with you, and just like you!

9

Using the Toilet

There are many ways to encourage your toddler to use the toilet. Introduce a toddler-size seat and low step to make the toilet more accessible. Or you and your toddler can shop for a potty chair to take home and try. Make toilet time appealing: offer a magazine to browse through or a tape for listening. Ask your librarian for a picture book on the subject; funny ones are especially welcome, such as Tony Ross's *I Want My Potty*.

Avoid making a fuss over accidents. Instead, reward use of the toilet with praise or even stars to pin up on a star chart. Other incentives may help, such as being able to wear nice underpants or the idea of being ready for nursery school. A slew of accidents may be a signal to slow down efforts or retreat to diapers for a while. Patience! Your toddler will use the toilet when she is ready. And as she practices, you can help her feel good about her body and its functions.

Bath Time

Toddlers tend to emerge from the tub not just cleaner, but calmer and cheerier as well. The chance for water play soothes and amuses most toddlers. Bathing is a good time for them to enjoy the way their bodies feel in water and to try washing themselves. Never leave the room when a toddler is in the tub; slipping in even a few inches of water can be dangerous.

There may be times when your toddler resists his bath. He may not want to interrupt what he is doing; he may fear the water or dislike having a shampoo. Try to be inventive and flexible.

HINTS   Let your toddler pick bath toys or choose a piece of clothing to wash in the tub.
Give him a choice of times to take a bath.

Try bubbles, shaped sponges, and soap body paint.
Sometimes just skip it!

11

Bedtime

Routines reassure toddlers. Presenting certain activities in prescribed order day after day shows that life has some predictability. When toddlers accept these events as routine — we brush our teeth every day — they are also more likely to cooperate. Set procedures at bedtime are very helpful; they offer toddlers a sense of security and the pleasure of experiencing something familiar at a time when they must separate from you.

HINTS ◆ Establish a bedtime and be consistent.
◆ Find a soothing way to end the day, whether with a bath, story, quiet song, or cuddle.

◆ Keep bedtime routines simple. Most toddlers want the entire ritual repeated each night.
◆ Be firm. Once your toddler is put to bed, she is to stay there. Mean it!

12

Feelings

Toddlers react to life intensely and spontaneously. They ride a roller coaster of feelings, laughing one minute, sobbing the next. They may feel shy in a strange setting, yet act sassy at home; vacillate between tenderness and jealousy toward a new sibling; develop fears of darkness or monsters, yet be fearless at great heights on the playground. They love with passionate hugs, feel rage with tumultuous kicks and screams.

HINTS ◆ Acknowledging and naming feelings helps your toddler begin to cope with a wide range of emotions.
◆ Offer acceptable ways for him to vent anger, such as punching cushions or Play-Doh.

◆ Encourage him to express his love and kindness.
◆ Remember that he's watching for cues; what do you do with your anger and affection? Teach him by your example!

13

No! No! No!

A toddler's first nos come as a shock, but they are her way of trying out independence, of saying, "I have the right to decide!" Every time a young child rejects your request, she feels her separateness and learns from your reactions what behavior you expect. As she grows surer of herself and her limits, she can choose to comply and say yes.

Offer your toddler safe opportunities to be autonomous, but be sure to set reasonable limits ("Yes, you may carry around that dish if you're careful, but not while you climb the stairs"). It's an ongoing search for that delicate balance.

HINTS ◆ Offer acceptable choices instead of just giving ultimatums.
◆ Use distraction. Simply change the subject from the object of your child's obstinacy to something else of interest to her.

◆ Instead of issuing a demand, invite desired behavior as part of a game or challenge.
◆ Phrase questions so they can't be answered with "No!"

14

Good-bye! Hello!

Letting go of each other is a gradual process that evolves each day from the moment your child is born. Look for ways to make separating easier. Explain where both you and your toddler will be while apart. A special routine to precede partings (and follow returns) can help, be it a story, song, or snuggle. State good-byes clearly and make them short. Even then, your toddler may cling to you one day, ignore you the next. You will have mixed emotions too. It's hard to feel completely satisfied, whether he's happy or sad to see you go. Focus on making the most of time you do have together.

HINTS Before going on a long trip without your toddler,

◆ record yourself singing his favorite songs so he can play the tape while you're away;
◆ hide a small surprise for each day of your absence (try cookies, toys, or stickers);

◆ put out family photographs;
◆ arrange to check in with baby-sitter and child by phone;
◆ post emergency phone numbers and instructions.

Then go and enjoy your time away!

Family

It is within the family that most children build self-esteem. Enjoy your toddler's company, let your enjoyment show, and she will feel loved. Hold her accountable for her actions, and she will feel responsible. Value your child, and she will feel valuable.

By what you say and do, you convey not only information but values. When the family is together, your toddler will observe how everyone behaves toward one another and will try to carve out a place for herself. By your clear, consistent reactions to your child, she gradually will learn what behavior you find desirable. For example, if you praise a toddler for helping out with a new baby, her generosity can become a source of pride.

Parents are a toddler's first teachers; your child is your disciple. What more important job is there?

17

Pretending

When your toddler offers you wooden-block "cookies" or growls that he's a tiger, you are witnessing his imagination emerge. Such pretend play is an absorbing pleasure for toddlers and serves as exercise in mental imagery, memory, and wish fulfillment. Your child's play reveals his current interests, fears, and passions.

Participating in your toddler's play can be a joy for you too. You can communicate ideas, feelings, values — and have fun. Moreover, acting "in character" can magically recruit your toddler's cooperation in completing tasks. Be careful not to intrude too much. Consider yourself a guest in his play and respect his right to reinvent the world as he chooses. It truly is a marvel to behold!

I'M A LITTLE TEAPOT, SHORT AND STOUT;
HERE IS MY HANDLE, HERE IS MY SPOUT.
WHEN I GET ALL STEAMED UP, HEAR ME SHOUT,
"TIP ME OVER AND POUR ME OUT!"

19

Friends

You needn't feel embarrassed about your toddler's lack of social graces. Most toddlers don't play cooperatively. They are too busy discovering that they are separate people; words like "me" and "mine" are still too new and irresistible. Toddlers do benefit from other children's company, however. They enjoy playing alongside them and learn from seeing what other youngsters do.

Don't always rush to intercede the moment a disagreement occurs between young children. If you demonstrate cooperation by sharing, taking turns, and showing compassion, eventually your toddler will follow your good example.

Song and Dance

Toddlers generally love music. Listening can be a shared or an independent activity; a familiar recording of children's songs sometimes provides just enough company when a toddler is ready for a few less-active minutes. Making music is even more fun! By this age, children begin to participate: singing bits of songs, dancing to rhythms, and accompanying melodies with simple instruments. Playing easy music games builds a toddler's listening skills. To teach volume, take turns singing a song loudly and then very softly. Vary a tune's pitch by using a high, squeaky voice or a low, grumbly one. Invent a short melody and invite your toddler to sing it back. Have her tap out a rhythm for you to repeat. Take advantage of music's wondrous ability to set a mood. Try singing a command to see if you get better cooperation. Doing so also helps keep you cheerful.

Easy Instruments to Make

DRUM

Turn a Quaker Oats box upside down; use a wooden spoon as the drumstick.

WOOD BLOCKS

Using tape or glue, cover two wood blocks with sandpaper; add screw-in knobs for handles.

TAMBOURINE

Decorate a paper plate and punch holes in its rim; attach jingle bells with ribbon or string.

SHAKER

Partly fill a plastic bottle with split peas; cap tightly and tape securely; decorate with child's artwork.

Arts and Crafts

It's not too early to expose your toddler to simple art materials. Set aside a place where your child can keep crayons, markers, stickers, paper, and chalk. Show him how to use glue and finger paint. Setting aside a space for messy work helps these projects go more smoothly. Keep in mind that the "doing" of art rather than its end product is what holds the real excitement at this age.

HINTS ◆ Take along crayons and paper for restaurants and waiting rooms.
◆ Encourage your toddler to make homemade greeting cards for family and friends.

◆ Remember that such basic skills as drawing a line or gluing down paper are real accomplishments for a toddler.
◆ Let your child know his artwork is beautiful.

PAT-A-CAKE, PAT-A-CAKE, BAKER'S MAN,
BAKE ME A CAKE AS FAST AS YOU CAN;
PAT IT AND PRICK IT, AND MARK IT WITH B,
PUT IT IN THE OVEN FOR BABY AND ME.

TEMPERA

sponge

brush

PAINT

potato

comb

A toddler can begin to appreciate her world and find beauty
in it if you stimulate and encourage her awareness.

HINTS ◆ Point out color, pattern, form,
and texture in all kinds of things: a smooth
stone, flowery dish, dark shadow, ragged leaf,
or shiny, red cherry.
◆ Look at pictures together in magazines,
catalogs, and books. Talking about art builds
her vocabulary.
◆ Try occasional trips to a gallery or an art
museum. Have your toddler search works of art
for animals, children, or something else she
likes. Then go home and let *her* do some art!

Reading

If you want a young child to love reading, then read to her often. Listening, she grows comfortable hearing written language and learns new words. She gets to handle books, examine them, smell them, and occasionally nibble them. Pick sturdy ones. Stories become friends as she meets all kinds of characters that broaden her world and help her understand herself.

Find ways for your toddler to participate: ask questions as you go along; teach her gestures that go with a rhyme. Use books to help introduce new experiences: an airplane trip, a birthday party, the arrival of a new sibling. Choose books of special interest to her. Narrations can be as personal as you like. You can speak in funny voices, add content to include your child, or shorten a story if interest flags. If you show that you enjoy reading, you'll find the pleasure is contagious!

24

Making TV Work

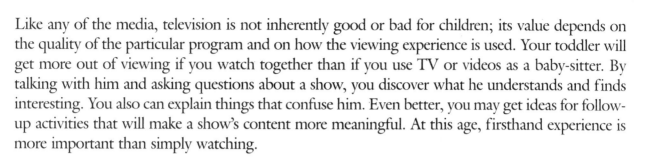

Like any of the media, television is not inherently good or bad for children; its value depends on the quality of the particular program and on how the viewing experience is used. Your toddler will get more out of viewing if you watch together than if you use TV or videos as a baby-sitter. By talking with him and asking questions about a show, you discover what he understands and finds interesting. You also can explain things that confuse him. Even better, you may get ideas for follow-up activities that will make a show's content more meaningful. At this age, firsthand experience is more important than simply watching.

25

Walk, Run, Climb, Jump!

Imagine how exciting it must be for toddlers — getting up on their own two feet for the first time and learning to maneuver through space! Find safe spaces where your child can practice running, climbing, and, later, jumping. Offer verbal support and guidance and be near enough to provide physical help. Set reasonable limits and suggest an acceptable alternative for a behavior you don't allow.

HINTS ◆ Structured exercise classes can be fun, especially if you both participate.
◆ Improvise games at home that call for your child to move in different ways: climbing over obstacles, racing to retrieve toys, throwing and catching, crawling like an animal.
◆ Pace activities to supply both active and quiet times.

Climbing down

Balancing

Ready... Set... Jump!

Whee! Sliding!

JUMP-JUMP-JUMP-JUMP OVER THE MOON;
JUMP ALL THE MORNING,
AND ALL THE NOON.

Tiptoe

Walking, walking—
pushing too!

Catch!

Kick!

Doing a somersault

Climbing
up

Walking backwards

Crawling

Alphabet

GREAT A, LITTLE a,
BOUNCING B,
THE CAT'S IN THE CUPBOARD
AND CAN'T SEE ME.

As a toddler gets older, you can begin to familiarize her with the alphabet. How much should you teach? Maybe many letters, maybe none. Let her interest in words and letter names be your guide. You might start with the first letter of her name. Point it out at opportune times: on a cereal box, in a book, on a road sign. Write it very large for her and write it very tiny. Say its sound with her. Moving her finger around a letter's outline in sand, on paper, or around a magnetic letter helps her to grasp its shape. When she can recognize one letter, introduce another, but continue to look for them both.

You needn't feel any pressure to instruct a toddler formally or to treat academic concepts differently from anything else you teach her. Whatever parts of the alphabet she picks up should come easily and give her satisfaction.

Can you find the letter M?

M! M for Mommy!

Numbers

Learning to count involves different skills. Reciting numbers in the proper order is one; some children begin to memorize the sequence as toddlers. Associating a number with the quantity of items to which it refers is another, more advanced skill; any amount greater than one is at first called two by most toddlers. A young child's progress with numbers includes making many mistakes; you need not correct every one. Trust that he will learn more and more, in time and with further instruction.

HINTS ◆ Offer information in small doses: if your toddler counts 1, 2, 3, and then adds numbers randomly, you might repeat his correct sequence and add just a 4.
◆ Describing things in terms of their numbers and counting during any activity helps acquaint toddlers with numbers and their uses.

Let's count! One, two, three ducks!

THE RAIN IS RAINING ALL AROUND,
IT FALLS ON FIELD AND TREE,
IT RAINS ON THE UMBRELLAS HERE,
AND ON THE SHIPS AT SEA.

Out in the Neighborhood

As long as you recognize that any trip away from home is eye-opening for a toddler, you will never lack for adventures. Playgrounds, libraries, and other public places that welcome children are valuable resources. Less obvious but no less interesting are bank errands, trips to the hardware store — virtually any shopping expedition. There are bags to hold, buttons to press, people to meet, and new sights and sounds to absorb.

HINTS ◆ Take along juice or milk and a snack or toy to help keep your toddler happy.
◆ Limit the number of stops.
◆ Slowing down your pace is apt to make going out nicer for you both.

◆ Assume that getting anywhere will take longer with a newly mobile toddler who wants to explore every direction except the one in which you're headed.

Animals

Toddlers are eager to visit animals, imitate their sounds, and learn about them. You can talk about where an animal lives, what it eats, how it moves, and what its young ones look like. It's fun to compare animal sizes, shapes, and colors; count legs or other body parts; and notice all kinds of physical characteristics. Picture books about animals are a big help.

To teach your toddler how to treat animals humanely, you yourself must show animals respect. Putting birdseed out after a snowfall or opening the window to free an insect will set valuable examples for him. You can also influence whether or not your child develops a fear of animals. Staying calm when you see a snake or spider will encourage your youngster to be interested in such creatures rather than afraid of them.

AN ELEPHANT GOES LIKE THIS AND THAT.
HE'S TERRIBLY BIG, AND HE'S TERRIBLY FAT.
HE HAS NO FINGERS, AND HE HAS NO TOES,
BUT GOODNESS GRACIOUS, WHAT A NOSE!

Traveling

When traveling long distances with your toddler, keep important items handy for feeding, clean-ups, naps, and play: diapers, wipes, change of clothes (for you too), blanket, drinks and food, playthings, books, and whatever "security" object your toddler has adopted for comfort. Scale down your provisions for short trips. Try taking along audiocassettes for entertainment in the car. To be well prepared and yet not overloaded with baggage is an art that comes with experience. Seize opportunities for your toddler to move about safely; being physically restricted is probably her greatest frustration during a long trip. Although traveling with a toddler may narrow your patience, it widens your child's experience tremendously.

Tractor

Fire Engine

Trucks

Motorcycle

Subway Train

Motorboat

Bicycle

Police Car

Wagon

THE WHEELS ON THE BUS GO ROUND AND ROUND,
ROUND AND ROUND, ROUND AND ROUND.
THE WHEELS ON THE BUS GO ROUND AND ROUND,
ALL THROUGH THE TOWN.

37

Health

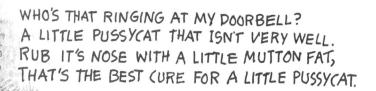

WHO'S THAT RINGING AT MY DOORBELL?
A LITTLE PUSSYCAT THAT ISN'T VERY WELL.
RUB IT'S NOSE WITH A LITTLE MUTTON FAT,
THAT'S THE BEST CURE FOR A LITTLE PUSSYCAT.

Treating a sick (and often cranky) toddler puts special demands on your attention, patience, and ability to make decisions. Administering medicine with decisiveness helps your child learn to accept it. Your child's pediatrician can recommend a health reference book if you want to keep one on hand, but don't hesitate to contact the doctor if you're ever unsure of what to do.

HINTS ◆ Keep up with your child's regular checkups to minimize illness.
◆ Introduce doctors in a positive way.
◆ Try not to expose youngsters unnecessarily to others who are sick, but expect even a healthy toddler to catch colds or flu.
◆ Look on the bright side: your child is building immunities with each infection he fights.

Safety

TWO LITTLE MONKEYS JUMPING ON THE BED,
ONE FELL OFF AND BUMPED HIS HEAD.
MOMMY CALLED THE DOCTOR
AND THE DOCTOR SAID,
"NO MORE MONKEYS JUMPING ON THE BED!"

Taking safety precautions can prevent accidents. Survey your home for potential hazards and move them out of your toddler's reach. Remember, with adult supervision toddlers *can* learn to handle objects safely. If an accident does occur, try to stay calm; only then can you assess an injury, treat it yourself or get help, and reassure your toddler that everything will be all right.

HINTS ◆ Put away such dangerous items as small, sharp pins and jewelry; toys with small, removable parts; mercury watch batteries; toxic cleansers, cosmetics, and similar poisonous substances; and telephones, lamps, and other heavy objects with dangling cords.
◆ Cover unused electrical outlets and make not touching plugs a rule.

◆ Install gates at both ends of open stairways.
◆ Turn pan handles on the stove to face inward.
◆ Be especially observant when visiting other people or when traveling.
◆ Keep handy a list of emergency phone numbers.
◆ Stock a child-proof medicine cabinet with first-aid supplies.

FIRST-AID SUPPLIES

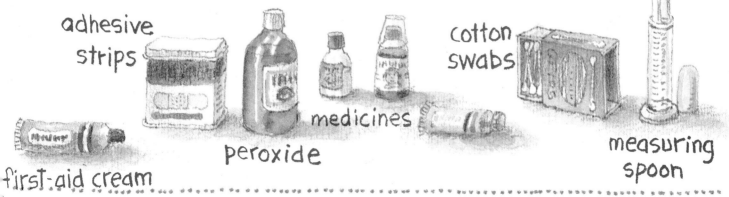

adhesive strips

cotton swabs

medicines

peroxide

first-aid cream

measuring spoon

Celebrate!

POLLY, PUT THE KETTLE ON,
POLLY, PUT THE KETTLE ON,
POLLY, PUT THE KETTLE ON,
WE'LL ALL HAVE TEA.

You don't have to wait for birthdays or national holidays to celebrate with your toddler: you can commemorate the arrival of spring, a welcome visitor, completed chores, good news — really, most anything! It takes so little to excite a toddler; a simple gesture such as lighting a candle and singing a song together can delight. These more personal, idiosyncratic festivities help cultivate a sense of family, especially when all members participate. You can invent a family tradition all your own by remembering to celebrate a particular occasion. Tuck away party hats, balloons, small presents, candles, and be spontaneous about merrymaking.

For a toddler,
every day is a celebration.

Join in!

GREAT A, LITTLE a,
BOUNCING B,
THE CATS IN THE CUPBOARD
AND CAN'T SEE ME.

THERE WAS A LITTLE GIRL
WHO HAD A LITTLE CURL
RIGHT IN THE MIDDLE OF HER FOREHEAD;
AND WHEN SHE WAS GOOD
SHE WAS VERY, VERY GOOD,
BUT WHEN SHE WAS BAD SHE WAS HORRID.

DOODLE, DOODLE, DOO,
THE PRINCESS LOST HER SHOE:
HER HIGHNESS HOPPED;
THE FIDDLER STOPPED,
NOT KNOWING WHAT TO DO.

WAKE UP, JACOB,
DAYS A-BREAKIN',
PEAS IN THE POT
AN' HOECAKE A-BAKIN'.

THE RAIN IS RAINING ALL AROUND,
IT FALLS ON FIELD AND TREE,
IT RAINS ON THE UMBRELLAS HERE,
AND ON THE SHIPS AT SEA.